BECOME THE NEXT MR. BEAST

A YOUTUBE CREATOR'S BLUEPRINT FOR VIRAL SUCCESS

LLOYD LEON

TABLE OF CONTENTS

CHAPTER 1

THE MR. BEAST PHENOMENON

What Makes Mr. Beast Tick?

What makes Mr. Beast tick? To truly understand the phenomenon that is Mr. Beast, one must delve into the unique concoction of passion, creativity, and a sprinkle of chaos that fuels his every move. His relentless pursuit of engaging content stems from an innate desire to entertain, inspire, and, above all, connect with his audience. He doesn't just create videos; he crafts experiences that invite viewers to participate in the fun. This playful energy draws people in, making them feel like they're part of something larger—something exciting and, quite frankly, a bit wild.

At the heart of Mr. Beast's success is his ability to blend philanthropy with entertainment. Watching him give away money, houses, and cars isn't just about the prizes; it's about the joy he spreads. This spirit of generosity resonates with viewers, transforming the act of watching a video into a positive experience. Aspiring creators can learn a valuable lesson here: infuse your content with purpose. Whether it's a challenge, a prank, or a heartfelt story, aim to leave your audience feeling uplifted. That emotional connection can be the secret sauce that keeps viewers coming back for more.

Creativity and innovation fuel Mr. Beast's content strategy. He's not afraid to push boundaries and think outside the box, constantly coming up with wild ideas that captivate his audience. From his outrageous challenges to his massive giveaways, each video feels fresh and exhilarating. Aspiring YouTubers should take notes—don't be afraid to experiment! Try out different formats, themes, and collaborations. The more you play with your content, the more likely you are to stumble upon that viral gem that catapults you into the limelight.

Collaboration is another key element of Mr. Beast's success. He often teams up with other creators, influencers, and friends, bringing diverse perspectives and ideas to his videos. This not only broadens his audience reach but also adds layers of fun and unpredictability to his content. For budding YouTubers, building relationships within the community is essential. Seek out fellow creators who share your passion and values. Together, you can brainstorm ideas and create memorable content that showcases each of your personalities while expanding your audience base.

Finally, Mr. Beast's understanding of analytics and audience engagement is top-notch. He pays close attention to what works and what doesn't, constantly refining his approach based on viewer feedback. This analytical mindset allows him to stay ahead of trends and maintain a strong connection with his fans. As an aspiring YouTuber, don't overlook the power of data. Dive into your analytics to discover what resonates with your audience. Use that information to tailor your content, ensuring it remains engaging and relevant. Embrace the playful spirit of experimentation, and you'll be well on your way to capturing the hearts of viewers just like Mr. Beast.

Analyzing the Success Formula

When diving into the whirlwind world of YouTube, it's essential to dissect what makes viral sensations like Mr. Beast tick. The success formula can be broken down into several key elements that aspiring creators should embrace. First and foremost, think of your content as a unique recipe. Start with the right ingredients: engaging storytelling, eye-catching thumbnails, and captivating titles that spark curiosity. Remember, the first impression is everything; you want viewers to click and stay glued to the screen. Just like Mr.

Beast's videos, your content should offer a tantalizing promise that viewers can't resist.

Next up is the importance of challenges and philanthropy. Mr. Beast's knack for creating jaw-dropping challenges not only entertains but also engages audiences in a way that feels participatory. Why not brainstorm your own zany challenge? Whether it's a 24-hour survival test in your backyard or surprising strangers with outrageous gifts, think big! Integrate a philanthropic angle, too. People love to see kindness and generosity in action. This not only amplifies your reach but also builds a community that rallies around shared values.

Engagement is the secret sauce that keeps viewers coming back for more. Create opportunities for your audience to interact with your content. Ask questions, encourage comments, and host polls to get your viewers involved. Building an engaging YouTube community isn't just about likes and shares; it's about fostering a sense of belonging. Mr. Beast excels at this with his fanbase, and you can too! Incorporate viewer feedback into your videos, respond to comments, and even feature fans in your content. Everyone loves to be acknowledged!

Collaboration is another powerful ingredient in the success formula. Partnering with other YouTubers can introduce your content to fresh audiences. Work with creators who share your values and audience demographics for maximum impact. Think of creative ways to merge your styles—maybe a challenge video or a fun Q&A session. When you join forces, you not only expand your reach but also enrich your content with diverse perspectives. Plus, your viewers will appreciate the novelty of seeing their favorite creators come together!

Lastly, let's not forget the importance of analytics in guiding your journey. Understanding YouTube analytics can feel like deciphering a secret code, but it's your treasure map to success. Dive into your metrics to discover what's working and what's not. Look for patterns in viewer engagement, watch time, and demographics to tailor your content accordingly. Use this data to refine your approach, experiment with new ideas, and keep evolving. By thoughtfully analyzing your performance, you'll be well on your way to crafting videos that resonate and inspire, just like Mr. Beast!

CHAPTER 2

CRAFTING YOUR VIRAL VIDEO STRATEGY

Understanding Trends and Timing

Understanding trends and timing is like catching the perfect wave in the ocean of YouTube. Just like surfers wait for that ideal swell, YouTubers need to be on the lookout for emerging trends that can catapult their content to viral heights. Start by immersing yourself in what's buzzing around you. Social media platforms, trending hashtags, and popular memes are just a few places where inspiration lurks. If you can spot a trend early, you can ride it to success, much like Mr. Beast does with his philanthropic challenges that often align with current events or trending topics.

Timing is equally crucial when it comes to releasing your content. Think of it as planning the perfect launch party: you wouldn't want to throw it on the same day as a major holiday or a big event that might steal your thunder. Pay attention to the cycles of your audience's engagement. For instance, if you're targeting a younger demographic, weekends or break times might be prime for posting. Utilize YouTube analytics to find out when your audience is most active, and then strike while the iron is hot. Remember, it's not just about creating great content; it's about making sure it gets the spotlight it deserves.

Let's not forget the power of collaboration. When a trend emerges, teaming up with other YouTubers can amplify your reach. Think of it as throwing a massive party where everyone brings their friends. By collaborating, you not only tap into each other's audiences but also create content that feels fresh and exciting. Look for creators who align with your brand and whose style complements yours. Together, you can brainstorm creative challenge ideas that resonate with current trends, making your content feel timely and relevant.

Engaging with your audience is another way to stay ahead of the game. When your community feels involved, they're more likely to share your content and contribute to its viral potential. Use polls, comments, and community posts to gauge what your viewers want to see next. You'd be amazed at how many fantastic ideas can come from your audience. This not only helps you understand their preferences but also fosters a sense of belonging, making them more likely to rally behind your next big video.

Finally, storytelling remains a timeless technique that can weave through all trends and timing strategies. Every viral video tells a compelling story, whether through humor, emotion, or unexpected twists. Even if you're jumping on a trend, infuse your unique narrative style into it. This personal touch will set you apart from the countless others trying to ride the same wave. As you hone your storytelling skills, you'll be able to create content that resonates long after the trend fades, ensuring your place in the ever-evolving landscape of YouTube.

The Power of Hooks and Thumbnails

In the bustling world of YouTube, where creativity reigns supreme, the first impression is often your ticket to success. Hooks and thumbnails are your golden keys, opening the door to an audience that's ready to engage, laugh, and maybe even cry with you. Think of your thumbnail as the cover of a book; it needs to be eye-catching enough that viewers can't resist clicking. A killer thumbnail paired with a hook that teases the best part of your video can be the difference between a thousand views and a million. So roll up your sleeves and get ready to master the art of visual allure!

Let's dive into the science of hooks. A great hook is like a magician's opening act—it captures attention and leaves your audience wanting more. Whether it's a bold statement, a shocking fact, or a tantalizing question, your hook should create curiosity faster than a cat chasing a laser pointer. Consider starting your videos with a bold claim, such as "I gave away $10,000 to strangers!" or a cliffhanger that makes viewers think, "What happens next?" This sets the stage for your storytelling and keeps viewers glued to their screens, waiting to see how everything unfolds.

Now, let's not forget about those thumbnails! They are your first line of defense against the overwhelming sea of content on YouTube. Experiment with bright colors, expressive faces, and large, bold text that screams, "Watch me!" Instead of just using a screenshot from your video, take the time to create a custom thumbnail that encapsulates the essence of your content. Use tools like Canva or Photoshop to whip up something that stands out. Remember, a thumbnail isn't just a pretty picture; it's a promise of the excitement that lies within your video.

As you craft your hooks and thumbnails, think about your target audience. What grabs their attention? What kind of content do they crave? Tap into their interests and preferences, and tailor your approach accordingly. If your audience loves challenges, then showcase that in your thumbnail and hook. If they're philanthropic, let them know how your video contributes to a cause they care about. Building a connection through your visual and verbal cues will not only enhance engagement but also help you foster a loyal community that eagerly awaits your next upload.

Finally, don't shy away from testing and iterating. Use YouTube Analytics to see which hooks and thumbnails resonate most with your audience. Sometimes, what you think will work might fall flat, while something you considered a throwaway could become a viral sensation. Embrace the playful experimentation inherent in content creation. With the right mix of creativity, boldness, and a little bit of trial and error, you'll be well on your way to creating content that's not just watched but shared, loved, and talked about—just like Mr. Beast himself!

CHAPTER 3

PHILANTHROPY AS A CONTENT CATALYST

Exploring the Impact of Giving

Giving is more than just a feel-good activity; it's a powerful tool that can launch your YouTube career into the stratosphere. When you create content that revolves around philanthropy, you tap into a deep well of goodwill and community engagement. This isn't just about donating money or time; it's about weaving generosity into the very fabric of your videos. Imagine your audience not just watching your content but becoming part of a movement, rallying behind a cause that resonates with them. The impact of giving can transform your channel from a simple entertainment platform into a beacon of hope and inspiration, making you the next Mr. Beast in no time.

Incorporating philanthropic themes into your videos can lead to viral success. Think of creative challenges that require your audience to participate in acts of kindness. How about a "Random Acts of Kindness Challenge" where viewers share their experiences? This not only engages your current audience but also attracts new subscribers who are eager to join in on the fun. By highlighting stories of people being helped, you create a narrative that's both heartwarming and shareable. The more people see your commitment to giving, the more they'll want to support you and your channel. Remember, the goal is to make your audience feel like they're part of something bigger.

Building an engaging YouTube community is all about fostering connections, and philanthropy can be the glue that holds it all together. When your viewers see that you care about making a difference, they're more likely to stick around and contribute to your mission. Encourage them to share their ideas on how to give back, and feature their suggestions in your videos. This not only promotes engagement but also makes your audience feel valued. They'll become your biggest champions, spreading the word about your content and helping you grow your channel organically.

Collaboration with other YouTubers can amplify your philanthropic efforts. Partner with fellow creators who share your passion for giving back, and brainstorm ideas for joint projects that can reach wider audiences. Whether it's a charity livestream, a donation drive, or a challenge video, working together can create a ripple effect that magnifies your impact. Plus, collaborating brings fresh perspectives and new ideas into the mix, keeping your content exciting and relevant. Your combined audiences will appreciate the effort, and you may even discover new friends in the YouTube community.

Lastly, don't underestimate the power of storytelling in your philanthropic content. Each act of giving has a story behind it, and sharing those tales can captivate your audience in ways that simple statistics cannot. Use your videos to showcase the people you're helping, the challenges they face, and the joy that comes from making a difference. This authentic approach not only enhances viewer engagement but also encourages them to take action themselves. As you harness the impact of giving, you'll not only be entertaining your audience but also inspiring them to join you on your journey, creating a legacy that goes far beyond YouTube.

How to Integrate Giving into Your Videos

Integrating giving into your videos isn't just a trend; it's a game changer for your channel and your community. Imagine starting your video with a bang, promising to donate a portion of the ad revenue to a charity that resonates with your audience. This not only sets a positive tone but also builds an instant connection with viewers who share those values. When they know that watching your content contributes to a good cause, they're more likely to engage, share, and come back for more. So, sprinkle that philanthropic magic into your content, and watch your community grow.

Now, let's get creative! Think about how you can weave giving into your challenges and collaborations. For instance, if you're doing a 24-hour challenge, why not add a twist where you donate a certain amount for every hour completed? Or, during a collaboration with another YouTuber, team up to raise funds for a local charity. The more fun and engaging the challenge, the more likely it is to go viral. Plus, your audience will feel like they're part of something bigger, turning views into a movement. This is the kind of energy that not only boosts your channel but also makes a real impact.

Don't forget about storytelling! People love stories, especially those that tug at the heartstrings. Share anecdotes of past donations or highlight the people who benefit from your giving. This could be a mini-documentary style segment where you show the impact of your contributions. By illustrating the effects of your generosity, you transform your videos from mere entertainment into inspiring narratives that resonate deeply. Remember, viewers are more likely to share your content if it inspires them, and stories of kindness and impact are the perfect catalyst.

Engaging your community is crucial, and involving them in your giving initiatives can make them feel valued. Consider running polls or challenges where your viewers can vote on which charity you should support next. You could even feature their suggestions in your videos! This interaction not only boosts viewer engagement but also fosters a sense of ownership. When your audience feels like they're part of the decision-making process, they're more likely to stick around and contribute, turning casual viewers into dedicated fans.

Finally, leverage social media to amplify your philanthropic efforts. Share behind-the-scenes moments on Instagram or TikTok, highlighting your giving journey. Create a hashtag for your initiative that encourages viewers to share their own acts of kindness. The more you promote the cause, the greater the sense of community you'll build. By integrating giving into your videos and beyond, you're not just creating entertaining content; you're establishing a legacy of generosity that could inspire countless others. So, get out there, spread the joy, and let your channel be a beacon of hope!

CHAPTER 4

BUILDING YOUR YOUTUBE COMMUNITY

Engaging with Your Audience

Engaging with your audience is like hosting a never-ending party where you're the life of the event. To channel your inner Mr. Beast, you need to create an atmosphere where your viewers feel not just like spectators, but integral members of your crew. Start by actively responding to comments and encouraging discussions, because nothing says "I value you" like a personalized shout-out. Make your audience feel special by acknowledging their contributions; a simple "Thank you for your idea!" can go a long way. Remember, every comment is a chance to build a connection, and every connection is a step closer to creating a loyal fanbase.

Now, let's sprinkle in some fun challenges and polls! Engage your followers by asking them to vote on what you should do next or which crazy stunt to attempt. This involvement not only provides you with fresh content ideas but also makes your audience feel like they're part of the action. The thrill of their choice coming to life can create a buzz that keeps them coming back for more. Plus, the excitement of anticipation builds a community around your content, making each video a mini-event that everyone looks forward to.

Another fantastic way to engage is through storytelling. Craft narratives that resonate with your viewers. Share your journey, your struggles, and your triumphs in a way that feels relatable and authentic. When your audience sees you as a real person with real experiences, they're more likely to stick around. Incorporate their stories into your content, showcasing their successes and challenges. This kind of interaction not only strengthens your bond but also fosters a sense of belonging, making everyone feel like they're part of an exclusive club.

Collaboration can also be a game-changer. Partnering with other YouTubers can introduce your channel to new audiences and create dynamic content that showcases different perspectives. Imagine hosting a challenge with another creator where both of your audiences can engage and interact. This cross-pollination of fan bases can lead to explosive growth, as viewers love to see their favorite creators working together. Plus, it's a great way to tap into fresh ideas and formats that can elevate your content to new heights.

Finally, don't underestimate the power of social media to amplify your engagement. Use platforms like Instagram, TikTok, and Twitter to share behind-the-scenes content, sneak peeks, and personal stories. This creates an additional layer of interaction with your audience. Encourage them to share their thoughts and experiences related to your content. The more you engage with them across various platforms, the stronger your community becomes. In this digital age, the more connected you are with your audience, the more likely they are to turn into loyal fans who can't wait to see what you do next.

Creating a Loyalty Loop

Creating a Loyalty Loop is like crafting the ultimate recipe for success on YouTube; it's all about mixing the right ingredients to keep your audience coming back for more. Imagine your viewers as loyal fans of a beloved series, eagerly awaiting the next episode. To create that kind of anticipation, you need to engage your audience consistently and meaningfully. Start by establishing a strong connection through your content. Use humor, relatability, and a sprinkle of your unique personality to draw them in. Share stories that resonate with their experiences, creating a bond that makes them feel like part of your journey.

Once you've hooked your audience, it's time to deepen that connection through interactive elements. Polls, challenges, and viewer shoutouts can transform passive viewers into active participants. When your fans feel like they have a stake in your content, they're more likely to stick around. Consider incorporating recurring segments in your videos where viewers can submit their ideas or vote on what they want to see next. This not only boosts engagement but also fosters a sense of community. When your audience feels valued and heard, they'll keep returning, eager to see if their contributions made the cut.

Don't forget to leverage the power of social media to reinforce your Loyalty Loop. Share behind-the-scenes content, sneak peeks of upcoming videos, or even host live Q&A sessions. This transparency helps demystify the content creation process and invites viewers into your world. Encourage them to share their thoughts and feedback on social platforms, making them feel like they're part of a lively conversation. The more you engage with them outside of YouTube, the more they'll feel a sense of loyalty to you and your brand.

In addition to interactive strategies, consider implementing a rewards system. This could be anything from shoutouts to exclusive content for your most dedicated fans. Gamifying the experience can elevate their level of commitment, making it exciting for them to engage with your channel. You could even create a tiered system that recognizes different levels of loyalty, giving fans something to aspire to. When viewers see that their efforts are acknowledged, they'll naturally want to become more involved, drawing others into the Loyalty Loop.

Finally, monitor your analytics to understand what keeps your audience hooked. Analyze which videos generate the most engagement and adapt your content strategy accordingly. By identifying trends, you can tailor your future videos to match your audience's preferences, ensuring they stay excited about what's coming next. The key is to stay flexible and responsive; just like in any good relationship, you need to listen and adapt. Creating a Loyalty Loop isn't just about gaining subscribers; it's about building a thriving community that champion your content and eagerly supports your journey to becoming the next Mr. Beast.

CHAPTER 5

COLLABORATING LIKE A PRO

Finding and Approaching Other Creators

Finding and approaching other creators can feel like stepping into a giant game of musical chairs—everyone's looking for a seat, but you want to make sure you snag the best one. The YouTube universe is packed with countless creators, each with their own unique flair and fanbase. So how do you sift through this sea of talent to find your perfect match? Start by exploring the niches that resonate with your own style. Whether it's gaming, challenges, or philanthropy, look for creators who align with your content and values. This isn't just about finding someone to collaborate with; it's about building connections that can elevate your content to the next level.

Once you've identified potential collaborators, it's time to break the ice. Approach them the way you'd slide into a DM—casually and with confidence. Craft a message that's fun and engaging, showcasing your personality while clearly expressing why you think a collaboration would be a blast. Mention specific videos of theirs that you enjoyed or ideas you have for working together. Remember, creators love to hear feedback, and this shows that you appreciate their work. Your enthusiasm will shine through and make you stand out from the crowd.

Now, let's talk about the art of pitching your collaboration ideas. When you reach out, be ready with a few creative concepts that blend both of your styles. Think outside the box! What if you combined a philanthropic challenge with a hilarious prank? Or maybe you could host a gaming tournament that raises funds for charity? The more unique and entertaining your idea, the better your chances of getting a yes. And don't forget to highlight the mutual benefits— how will both of you grow from this partnership? This is not just about you; it's a teamwork dream!

When you finally team up, keep the energy high and the communication open. Collaboration is like a dance; you want to make sure you're both in sync. Share your thoughts, be flexible, and encourage each other's creative input. This is your moment to create something special together, so be sure to have fun with it! The more enjoyable the process, the more likely your audience will feel that excitement too. Remember, authenticity is key, so let your personalities shine through in the content you create.

After the collaboration wraps up, don't let the connection fizzle out. Continue to support each other by engaging with their content and sharing their work with your audience. This not only strengthens your relationship but also encourages your followers to check out their channel. Plus, who knows? You might discover new opportunities for future collaborations! Keep the momentum going, and you'll find that the YouTube community is a vibrant playground filled with endless possibilities for growth and success.

Maximizing Collaborative Content

Maximizing collaborative content is your golden ticket to skyrocketing your YouTube channel into the stratosphere of viral success! Think of collaboration as a fun party where everyone brings their own unique flavor, and together, you cook up something unforgettable. YouTube is a vast playground, and teaming up with fellow creators not only diversifies your content but also exposes you to their audience. This means more eyeballs on your videos, and who doesn't want that? So, grab your camera and get ready to make some friends because collaborating is where the magic begins.

To kick things off, consider the niches of your potential collaborators. Aligning with creators who share your passion or whose audience would enjoy your content can lead to explosive growth. Let's say you're all about philanthropy, just like Mr. Beast. Partnering with another YouTuber who thrives on doing good can amplify your message and make a bigger impact. Imagine pooling your resources to build a massive charity event, and then capturing every heartwarming moment on camera. Not only will it be epic, but it'll also create a powerful storyline that resonates with viewers and gets them sharing like crazy.

Don't forget the importance of creative challenges! These are like the sprinkles on your collaboration cupcake. Spice things up by incorporating fun and engaging challenge ideas that both you and your collaborator can participate in. Whether it's a crazy obstacle course or a charitable scavenger hunt, the excitement will be infectious. Your audience will love watching you tackle these challenges together, and they'll be eager to jump in on the fun, too. Challenges create a dynamic viewing experience, fostering a sense of community and encouraging viewers to engage through comments and shares.

Now, let's chat about the power of social media. Once your collaborative masterpiece is ready to drop, blast it out on all your platforms. Use Instagram, Twitter, TikTok, and even good old-fashioned Facebook to create buzz around your collaboration. Tease snippets of the content, share behind-the-scenes moments, and invite your followers to join the conversation. This cross-promotion not only drives traffic to your video but also builds anticipation, ensuring even more viewers tune in once it's live. Remember, the more noise you make, the more people will want to be part of your fun!

Finally, don't underestimate the magic of storytelling. When you collaborate, you're not just creating content; you're crafting a narrative that draws viewers in. Share your experiences, the challenges you faced, and the laughs you had along the way. Make it relatable and engaging! Your audience wants to feel connected, and a well-told story will keep them coming back for more. By maximizing collaborative content through thoughtful partnerships, exciting challenges, social media buzz, and compelling storytelling, you'll be well on your way to becoming the next Mr. Beast. So gear up, get creative, and let the collaborations roll!

CHAPTER 6

SOCIAL MEDIA: YOUR
SECRET WEAPON

Choosing the Right Platforms

Choosing the right platforms to amplify your YouTube content is like picking the perfect stage for a grand performance. You've got your main act—YouTube, of course—but don't underestimate the power of supporting platforms. Think of social media as your hype crew: they're there to build excitement, share snippets, and drive traffic to your channel. Platforms like Instagram, TikTok, and Twitter can help you create a buzz that translates into more views and subscribers. When you strategically use these platforms, you can capture attention even before the main event rolls out on YouTube.

Now, let's talk about where your audience hangs out. If your niche is all about philanthropy like Mr. Beast, platforms where people are passionate about giving back, such as Facebook Groups or charity-focused Reddit threads, can be goldmines. For challenge videos, TikTok is a playground where trends explode overnight. Understanding where your potential viewers are chilling will help you tailor your content and engage with them effectively. Think of it like a treasure map—follow it to find your audience, and they'll follow you back to your YouTube channel.

Engagement is the name of the game! While YouTube is your home base, engaging with your community on other platforms can turn casual viewers into loyal fans. Share behind-the-scenes content, sneak peeks of upcoming videos, or even just fun polls to get your audience involved. The more they feel like part of the journey, the more likely they are to share your content and spread the word. Remember, it's not just about numbers; it's about creating a vibrant, interactive community that thrives on your energy.

Collaboration is another key element in your platform strategy. Working with other creators can open doors to new audiences and unique content ideas. Find creators in similar niches and brainstorm ways to cross-promote on each other's platforms. A fun Instagram Live chat, a TikTok challenge, or even a collaborative YouTube video can create a ripple effect, bringing in new subscribers who are eager to see what you're all about. Collaboration isn't just about sharing viewers; it's about creating unforgettable moments that resonate with audiences.

Lastly, don't forget to analyze and adapt! Keep an eye on what platforms are driving the most traffic to your YouTube channel. Use analytics tools to track engagement and see which content types resonate best across different platforms. By constantly evaluating your strategy, you can pivot and focus your energy where it counts the most. Choose your platforms wisely, mix in some creativity, and watch as your YouTube community grows, all while having a blast along the way!

Crafting Shareable Content

Crafting shareable content is like cooking up a viral recipe that everyone wants a taste of. It's all about creating videos that people can't help but click on, watch, and share with their friends. To start, think about what excites you and your audience. Whether it's outrageous challenges, heartwarming acts of kindness, or mind-blowing tutorials, your passion will seep through the screen. When you're genuinely excited about your content, it radiates to viewers, prompting them to share that energy with their circles.

Next, keep the magic of storytelling in mind. Each video should have a clear arc that hooks viewers from the start. Think of it as a mini-movie where you can introduce a conflict or challenge, build tension, and deliver a satisfying resolution. This structure not only keeps your audience engaged but also encourages them to share your video as a must-watch experience. Incorporate elements that resonate with your viewers' emotions; laughter, surprise, and even a few tears can fuel the shareability of your content.

Visual appeal is another critical ingredient in your shareable content recipe. Bright colors, dynamic editing, and eye-catching thumbnails are essential for grabbing attention. You want your video to stand out in a sea of content, especially on platforms like YouTube and social media. Experiment with different styles and formats that reflect your unique brand. The more visually engaging your content is, the more likely viewers will feel compelled to share it with their friends or post it on their own channels.

Engagement doesn't stop with just creating great content; it's essential to build a community around it. Encourage viewers to comment, share their thoughts, and even participate in upcoming challenges. Create a sense of belonging where your audience feels valued and heard. When people feel connected to a creator, they're far more likely to share their content. Consider running giveaways or challenges that require audience participation to boost interaction and spread your content even further.

Lastly, leverage the power of collaboration with other YouTubers. By teaming up with creators in your niche or even those outside of it, you can tap into their audiences and widen your reach. Collaborations can lead to exciting content that showcases each creator's strengths, and when their viewers see the fun you're having together, they'll want to share that excitement. Remember, shareable content thrives on community, connection, and creativity, so keep experimenting and pushing the boundaries of what's possible!

CHAPTER 7

CHALLENGE YOUR
CREATIVITY

Brainstorming Unique Challenge Ideas

Brainstorming unique challenge ideas can be the secret sauce that propels your YouTube channel into the viral stratosphere. Think outside the box and let your imagination run wild. Start by considering unusual settings or themes that haven't been overdone. For instance, instead of the standard "24-hour challenge," how about a "24-hour challenge in a haunted house" or "24-hour challenge in a zero-gravity environment"? The more outlandish and exciting the premise, the more likely it is to capture attention and spark interest.

Next, tap into current trends and popular culture. What's hot right now? Is there a viral meme, a trending dance, or a popular movie that everyone's buzzing about? Incorporating these elements into your challenges can give them a fresh twist. For example, you could create a challenge that combines a popular TikTok dance with a physical obstacle course. This not only makes for great content but also connects your video to something that viewers are already excited about, increasing the chances of it going viral.

Don't shy away from involving your audience in the brainstorming process. Social media can be a treasure trove of ideas. Pose questions, run polls, or host brainstorming sessions on platforms like Twitter or Instagram. Your subscribers might have some wild and wonderful ideas that you hadn't considered. Plus, engaging with them in this way builds your community and makes them feel invested in the content you create. Remember, the more fun and creative the challenge, the more likely your viewers will want to participate and share it.

Consider collaboration with other YouTubers to spark unique challenges. Partnering with creators from different niches can lead to some unexpected and entertaining results. Imagine a cooking challenge with a gamer, or a fitness challenge with a beauty influencer. The contrast can create dynamic content that attracts viewers from both communities, amplifying your reach and engagement. Plus, it's a fantastic way to forge relationships and build a supportive network within the YouTube community.

Finally, don't forget the philanthropic angle. Challenges that incorporate giving back can resonate deeply with audiences. Think about creating challenges where the stakes involve donations to charity or community service. For instance, for every task completed, you could pledge a certain amount to a charitable cause. This not only adds a layer of meaning to your content but also encourages viewers to contribute and share your video, amplifying your message and potentially leading to viral success.

Executing Challenges with Flair

Executing challenges with flair is where the magic happens on YouTube. Imagine setting up a wild challenge that not only entertains your audience but also leaves a lasting impression. The key to success lies in creativity and presentation. Think outside the box—whether it's a massive obstacle course in your backyard or a quirky food challenge with a twist, the more unexpected, the better. Your viewers are constantly searching for fresh content, so don't be afraid to take risks. A unique concept paired with your personal touch can turn a simple challenge into a viral sensation.

Next, let's talk about the execution. It's not just about what you do; it's how you do it. Keep your energy high, and don't shy away from a bit of theatrics. Your viewers should feel like they're part of the experience, cheering you on from the sidelines. Use engaging visuals, catchy music, and clever editing to amp up the excitement. Incorporate humor and surprises along the way to keep your audience on their toes. Remember, the more entertaining you are, the more likely your challenge will be shared, leading to that viral moment you're striving for.

Incorporating philanthropic elements can elevate your challenges to new heights. Imagine hosting a challenge where every milestone reached translates into donations for a worthy cause. Not only does this add a layer of meaning to your content, but it also encourages viewers to engage and share for a good cause. People love to support creators who give back, and it builds a stronger bond with your audience. Plus, it sets you apart from the sea of challenge videos flooding YouTube.

Collaboration is another secret ingredient for executing challenges with flair. Partnering with fellow YouTubers can amplify your reach and introduce your content to new audiences. Imagine teaming up with a creator who has a completely different style or niche—this can lead to some truly entertaining and unpredictable challenges. The dynamic between you and your collaborator can create a natural chemistry that viewers love to watch. Plus, the combined resources can elevate the production quality of your challenge, making it even more appealing.

Finally, don't forget to analyze the results of your challenges. After the dust settles, dive into your YouTube analytics to see what resonated with your viewers. Did certain elements lead to higher engagement? Were there moments that spurred more shares or comments? Understanding your audience's reaction will help you refine your future challenges. Keep experimenting and iterating based on feedback and data. The more you learn, the better equipped you'll be to execute even more impressive challenges with flair in the future.

CHAPTER 8

MONETIZATION MASTERY

Exploring Revenue Streams

In the wild world of YouTube, revenue streams are like treasure chests waiting to be unlocked. If you want to follow in the footsteps of Mr. Beast, you need to think creatively about how to bring in those sweet, sweet dollars. Sure, ad revenue is the classic route, but why stop there? Embrace diverse income sources like merchandise sales, sponsorships, and even fan funding. Imagine having your own line of quirky T-shirts or exclusive merchandise that your fans can't resist! By mixing and matching these revenue streams, you'll not only pad your pockets but also keep your community engaged and excited about supporting your brand.

Speaking of community, let's dive into the goldmine of fan funding. Platforms like Patreon and Ko-fi allow your most dedicated followers to support your endeavors financially in exchange for exclusive content or perks. This not only strengthens the bond between you and your audience but also provides a steady stream of income that isn't reliant on the fickle nature of ad revenue. Consider hosting special Q&A sessions, behind-the-scenes content, or even personalized shout-outs for your patrons. By rewarding your fans for their support, you'll create an ecosystem where everyone feels like they're part of something bigger—just like Mr. Beast's epic challenges that unite fans in excitement.

Don't forget about collaborations! Partnering with other YouTubers can not only introduce you to new audiences but also open up unique monetization opportunities. Think of it as a fun game of tag where everyone benefits. You can create joint content, share sponsorship deals, or even run competitions that engage both of your audiences. The synergy of two creators coming together can result in explosive growth and revenue potential. Plus, who doesn't love a good collaboration video? They can be a delightful mix of creativity and chaos, just like some of Mr. Beast's most unforgettable moments!

Now, let's talk about the power of storytelling, which can be a driving force behind your revenue streams. Crafting compelling narratives not only keeps viewers glued to their screens but also makes them more likely to support your channel financially. Whether it's a heartwarming tale of giving back to the community or an exhilarating challenge that leaves them on the edge of their seats, your storytelling prowess will enhance viewer engagement. When people connect emotionally with your content, they're much more inclined to share it, contribute to your Patreon, or buy that limited-edition merch. Remember, a well-told story can turn casual viewers into loyal fans and financial supporters.

Lastly, understanding YouTube analytics is like having a treasure map that guides you to uncover the most lucrative opportunities. By analyzing which videos resonate with your audience, you can tailor your content to maximize engagement and revenue potential. Pay attention to metrics such as watch time, audience demographics, and engagement rates. This information can help you refine your content strategy and tap into what works best for your niche. Just like Mr. Beast, who knows exactly what keeps his fans coming back for more, you too can use analytics to navigate the ever-changing landscape of YouTube and ensure your revenue streams flow like a river of gold.

Balancing Monetization and Authenticity

Balancing monetization and authenticity is like walking a tightrope while juggling flaming torches—exciting but a bit nerve-wracking. As YouTubers aspiring to follow in the footsteps of viral giants like Mr. Beast, you face the constant temptation to cash in on your content. The allure of brand deals and ad revenue can easily overshadow the genuine connection you build with your audience. But remember, viewers can sniff out inauthenticity faster than you can say "collaboration." Striking the right balance ensures that your content remains true to your brand while still raking in those sweet, sweet dollars.

First off, keep your core values front and center. What made you start creating content in the first place? Was it a passion for entertaining, educating, or inspiring? Always revisit those roots, because they are your North Star. When monetization opportunities come knocking, ask yourself: does this align with my message? If the answer is a resounding "yes," then go ahead and embrace that partnership! But if it feels off-brand or forced, it's time to say "thanks, but no thanks." Your audience appreciates authenticity, and they'll reward you for it with their loyalty.

Next, get creative with your monetization strategies. Instead of relying solely on traditional ads or sponsorships, think outside the box! Consider launching a merchandise line that reflects your unique style or creating exclusive content for a Patreon community. This not only diversifies your income streams but also deepens your connection with your audience. They'll appreciate the chance to support you in a way that feels personal and authentic. Plus, it gives you more freedom to create without the pressure of hitting specific ad revenue goals.

Engaging with your community is another vital aspect of maintaining authenticity. Regularly interact with your audience through comments, social media, and live streams. This two-way communication fosters a sense of belonging and shows that you genuinely care about their opinions. When your viewers feel like they are part of a community, they are more likely to support you financially. They'll want to see you succeed, and that means buying your merch or supporting your channels. It's a win-win situation where everyone feels valued and connected.

Lastly, remember that storytelling is your superpower. Whether you're crafting a heartwarming challenge or sharing a philanthropic endeavor, weave narratives that resonate with your audience. Highlight your genuine intentions behind monetization efforts, such as reinvesting into your content or supporting charitable causes. When viewers see that their support directly contributes to something meaningful, they're more likely to rally behind you. Balancing monetization with authenticity isn't just a strategy; it's a way to build a legacy that reflects your true self while achieving viral success.

CHAPTER 9

STORYTELLING THAT CAPTIVATES

The Elements of a Great Story

Every great story starts with a hook, and for YouTubers, that hook is everything. Imagine scrolling through YouTube and stumbling upon a video that grabs your attention in the first five seconds. That's the magic of a captivating introduction! Whether it's a jaw-dropping stunt or a quirky question that makes viewers think, your opening needs to be a showstopper. Think of it as a rollercoaster ride; you want to pull them in with a thrilling ascent before the exhilarating drop. The more unexpected and amusing your hook is, the better your chances of enticing viewers to stick around for the entire ride.

Next up, we have characters—those lovable personalities that viewers can't help but root for. In the realm of YouTube, this can be you, your friends, or even your pets! The key is to create relatable characters that resonate with your audience. Show them your quirks, your triumphs, and even your failures. Authenticity breeds connection, and when your viewers feel like they know you, they're more likely to come back for more. So, whether you're pulling off a crazy challenge or giving away a car, let your true self shine through. Make them laugh, make them cry, but above all, make them feel!

Conflict is what keeps the story moving, and in the world of YouTube, that can take many forms. Think of the challenges you face while creating content—budget constraints, time limitations, or even dealing with the occasional technical glitch. By sharing these challenges with your audience, you not only create drama but also build suspense. Will you succeed in your latest challenge, or will you face a hilarious setback? This element adds depth to your story, making it relatable and engaging. Remember, every great journey has its bumps in the road, and sharing those moments can turn a simple video into a memorable adventure.

Now, let's talk about resolution—the sweet reward at the end of your narrative. This is where you tie everything together, delivering on the promise you made in your hook. Whether it's the triumphant moment of completing a challenge or the heartwarming reaction of a charity recipient, resolution is where the magic happens. It's your chance to make your viewers feel good, and perhaps even inspire them to take action. Leave them with a sense of satisfaction, a smile on their face, or a burning desire to share your video with friends. The resolution is your victory lap, so make it count!

Lastly, let's not forget the importance of community. A great story doesn't just end with the video; it continues in the comments, the likes, and the shares. Engage your audience by asking for their opinions, inviting them to join in on challenges, or even featuring their reactions in your next video. Building a community around your storytelling not only enhances your content but also fosters loyalty among your viewers. Remember, YouTube is a two-way street, and the more you involve your audience, the more invested they'll become in your journey. So go on, spin your tale, and watch as your community blossoms!

Techniques for Engaging Narratives

Engaging narratives are the secret sauce that can turn a simple video into a viral masterpiece. When crafting your content, think of storytelling as your trusty sidekick. Begin with a hook that grabs attention faster than a cat video on a lazy afternoon. Whether it's a jaw-dropping challenge, an unexpected twist, or a heartwarming moment, your opening should be so captivating that viewers can't help but click "play" and keep watching. Remember, the first few seconds are like the first impression at a party—make it count!

Once you've snagged their attention, it's time to build your narrative like a rollercoaster ride. Introduce characters, whether they are friends, family, or even your pet goldfish, and create a relatable scenario that draws viewers into your world. Use humor, surprise, and a sprinkle of drama to keep the energy high. The key is to ensure that your audience feels an emotional connection. When they care about the outcome, they're more likely to engage with your content and share it with their friends, creating an organic ripple effect.

Don't forget the importance of pacing! Just like in a good book, the rhythm of your story matters. Mix up your shots, switch between wide angles and close-ups, and use fast cuts to maintain excitement. When you introduce challenges or philanthropic elements, make sure to build tension leading up to the big reveal. This can be as simple as a countdown or a series of mini-climaxes that keep viewers on the edge of their seats. The more invested they are in your journey, the more likely they are to stick around to the end.

Visual storytelling is just as crucial as the spoken word. Use engaging visuals, graphics, and on-screen text to enhance your narrative. Whether you're showcasing the heartwarming moments of your latest charity event or the thrilling chaos of a challenge, let the visuals complement your storytelling. And don't shy away from using humor or quirky animations to add personality. Remember, your video should be a feast for the eyes, keeping viewers entertained while they absorb your message.

Finally, wrap up your narrative in a way that resonates. A solid conclusion not only ties everything together but also encourages viewers to interact. Ask them to share their thoughts in the comments, challenge them to participate in your next endeavor, or inspire them to take action for a cause you care about. By leaving your audience with a clear call to action, you're not just ending a video; you're inviting them into a community where they feel valued and engaged. And that, my fellow creators, is how you turn casual viewers into loyal fans!

CHAPTER 10

DECODING YOUTUBE ANALYTICS

Key Metrics to Track

When you're on the quest to become the next Mr. Beast, keeping an eye on the right metrics is like having a treasure map in your back pocket. First up, let's talk about views. Views are the lifeblood of your channel, the shiny gold coins that indicate whether your content resonates with viewers. But don't just chase the numbers for the sake of it. Pay attention to where those views are coming from. Are they tuning in from your latest collaboration video? Or did a clever title snag their attention? Understanding the source of your views can help you craft future content that keeps your audience glued to their screens.

Next on the list is watch time. This is where the magic happens; it's not just about getting people to click on your video, but keeping them around for the ride. YouTube rewards channels that can hold viewers' attention, so track your average view duration. If viewers are dropping off after the first minute, it might be time to spice things up! Consider using engaging storytelling techniques or incorporating some of those wild challenge ideas that keep people hooked. Remember, if your audience is enjoying what they see, they're more likely to share it, and that's the ultimate goal!

Engagement metrics are another golden nugget worth tracking. Likes, comments, and shares are essentially the applause your content receives. High engagement means viewers are not just watching; they're actively participating in your channel. Encourage this interaction by asking questions, inviting suggestions, or even featuring fan comments in your videos. This not only builds community but also gives you insight into what your audience loves most. Who knows? Your next big video idea could come straight from a comment!

Let's not forget about subscriber growth. This is your channel's fan club, and every new subscriber is a vote of confidence in your content. Track not only how many subscribers you gain but also how many you lose. If you notice a dip, take a moment to analyze what might've caused it. Was it a controversial video? Or did you stray too far from what initially attracted your audience? Staying in tune with your subscribers ensures that you're not just throwing content into the void but creating videos that keep people coming back for more.

Lastly, don't overlook the power of social media metrics. Platforms like Instagram, Twitter, and TikTok can amplify your YouTube presence. Track how your posts drive traffic to your videos and how they contribute to your overall brand identity. Engaging with your community across these platforms can create a loyal fan base that carries over to your YouTube channel. So, while you're busy dreaming up your next big philanthropic stunt, remember to keep your eyes on these key metrics. They're the breadcrumbs that will lead you to viral success!

Using Data for Growth

Using data to fuel your growth on YouTube is like having a treasure map that leads you to your next big adventure. YouTube analytics might sound boring, but think of it as your secret weapon. Dive into those numbers, and you'll discover what your audience loves, what makes them click, and what keeps them coming back for more. The key is to study the trends and patterns in your views, watch time, and engagement rates. This is where you spot the golden nuggets—those videos that exploded in popularity or the moments that got your viewers chatting in the comments.

Once you've unearthed this data, the real fun begins. Use it to craft your future content! If your audience went wild over a challenge video, why not create a sequel or a spin-off? Or if a particular style of storytelling resonated with viewers, lean into that! Data isn't just numbers; it's a map of your audience's desires. Play around with formats, tweak your thumbnails, and experiment with titles based on what's worked before. Just like Mr. Beast, who thrives on innovative ideas, your creative juices should flow from what your audience craves.

Building an engaging YouTube community is another area where data plays a starring role. Pay attention to your comments section—your most passionate viewers are giving you direct feedback. Use polls, ask questions, and be proactive in figuring out what your community wants to see. Not only does this foster engagement, but it also shows your audience that you care about their input. When viewers feel heard, they're more likely to stick around and boost your channel's growth.

Collaboration is a powerful strategy, and data can guide you in choosing the right partners. Analyze other creators in your niche—who has a similar audience, and what kind of content do they produce? Working with others can introduce your channel to new viewers, and data can help ensure that your collabs are mutually beneficial. You don't want to team up with someone whose style doesn't align with yours; instead, find creators who complement your brand and bring something unique to the table.

Finally, don't forget to leverage social media with the insights you've gathered. Share snippets of your videos, behind-the-scenes content, and engage with your followers using the data you've collected about what resonates with them. Use platforms like Instagram, Twitter, and TikTok to amplify your reach. Experiment with different types of posts and stories to see what gets the most interaction. By tracking these interactions, you'll gain even more insight into your audience's preferences, creating a loop of growth that keeps your channel thriving. Data isn't just for the tech geeks; it's your ticket to becoming the next Mr. Beast!

CHAPTER 11

BUILDING YOUR BRAND IDENTITY

Defining Your Unique Voice

Finding your unique voice is like discovering the secret sauce that sets your YouTube channel apart from the rest of the buffet. In a world where everyone is vying for attention, being authentic is your ticket to viral fame. Think about it: when you watch a Mr. Beast video, what grabs your attention? It's not just the wild challenges or jaw-dropping stunts; it's his undeniable personality that shines through every frame. To become the next Mr. Beast, you need to harness that same energy and infuse it into your own content.

Start by reflecting on what makes you, well, you! What are your quirks, passions, and interests? Are you the jokester who can turn any situation into a laugh, or perhaps the one with a heart of gold who loves spreading kindness? This self-discovery process isn't just about finding your style; it's about understanding what resonates with your audience. Your unique voice should echo through every video, creating a familiar tune that viewers can't help but come back to. Embrace your individuality—it's your biggest asset!

Once you've identified your voice, it's time to sprinkle it liberally across your channel. Whether you're teaching your audience how to pull off an epic prank or sharing your latest philanthropic venture, let your personality shine through. Use humor, storytelling, or even dramatic flair, depending on what feels right for you. This is your chance to engage with viewers on a deeper level. When people connect with your authentic self, they're more likely to subscribe, share, and join your growing community.

Collaboration can also amplify your unique voice. Teaming up with fellow YouTubers allows you to explore new styles and ideas while still staying true to yourself. Choose partners who complement your vibe and share your passion for creating. This not only broadens your audience reach but also helps you learn from each other. Just remember, when you collaborate, your unique voice should still be at the forefront. It's like mixing different flavors in a smoothie—you want a delicious blend, not a muddled mess!

Lastly, don't forget to keep evolving. Your unique voice is not set in stone; it's more like clay that you can mold over time. As you grow and learn from your experiences, your content will naturally evolve, reflecting your journey as a creator. Stay open to feedback, experiment with different formats, and always be willing to adjust your approach. By staying true to your unique voice while embracing change, you'll not only captivate your audience but also pave the way for viral success just like Mr. Beast!

Visual Branding Essentials

Visual branding is the secret sauce that can elevate your YouTube channel from ordinary to extraordinary. Think of it as your channel's personality, the eye-catching elements that make people stop scrolling and start watching. From your channel art to your thumbnails, every visual aspect plays a crucial role in grabbing attention and conveying your unique style. Mr. Beast didn't become a household name just by luck; his visuals are as bold and memorable as his content. So, how can you harness the power of visual branding to create a channel that stands out in the crowded YouTube landscape?

First up, let's talk about your logo and channel art. This is your brand's first impression, and we all know how important that is! Your logo should be simple yet recognizable, something that viewers can instantly associate with your content. Channel art is your digital billboard—make sure it reflects your personality and niche. Whether you're a challenge master or a philanthropic powerhouse, your visuals should scream, "This is me!" Use vibrant colors and fun fonts that resonate with your audience and create a cohesive look that ties everything together.

Now, onto thumbnails—the real MVP when it comes to attracting clicks. Your thumbnails should be loud, proud, and packed with personality. They need to tell a story at a glance, enticing viewers to click on your video. Use bold text and striking images to create curiosity and hype. Think about Mr. Beast's thumbnails; they're not just pretty pictures; they're a promise of excitement and entertainment. Experiment with different styles, but always keep your brand colors and fonts consistent to build recognition over time.

Consistency is key in visual branding. Establish a style guide for your channel that outlines your color palette, fonts, and imagery. This creates a signature look that viewers will come to associate with your brand. Even in your videos, keep the visuals cohesive—use similar graphics, overlays, and transitions to create a seamless viewing experience. This not only enhances your branding but also keeps viewers engaged, making them more likely to subscribe and return for more.

Finally, don't forget to leverage social media for your visual branding! Share snippets of your videos, behind-the-scenes content, and engaging graphics that reflect your style. Platforms like Instagram and Twitter are perfect for showcasing your personality and connecting with your audience on a more personal level. Remember, your visual branding should extend beyond YouTube; it's about creating a holistic experience that resonates with viewers wherever they find you. So, get creative, have fun, and let your visual branding shine as brightly as your content!

CHAPTER 12

THE ROAD AHEAD

Adapting to Changes in the Platform

Adapting to changes in the platform is like surfing a wave; it requires balance, skill, and a keen eye for what's happening. YouTube, with its ever-shifting algorithms and trends, can feel like a wild ride. One minute, a new challenge is trending, and the next, it's yesterday's news. To become the next Mr. Beast, you need to be ready to pivot at a moment's notice. Keep your ear to the ground and your eyes on the screen; understanding these changes will be your secret weapon in the battle for viral success.

Start by paying attention to YouTube's updates and announcements. They often roll out new features that can enhance your content or help you reach a broader audience. For instance, when YouTube introduced Shorts, savvy creators jumped on the trend, producing bite-sized videos that captured attention and drove engagement. Embrace these changes and experiment with new tools and formats. Your willingness to adapt will not only keep your content fresh but also position you as a forward-thinking creator in the eyes of your audience.

Engaging with your community is another fantastic way to adapt. Your subscribers can be a treasure trove of insights. Ask them what they want to see next or what they think about recent changes on the platform. This open dialogue creates a sense of belonging and transforms your viewers into active participants in your journey. Plus, you might stumble upon a goldmine of ideas that align perfectly with current trends. Remember, the more you listen, the better you'll be at creating content that resonates with your audience.

Collaboration is an essential component of adapting to YouTube's landscape. Partnering with other creators can open doors to new audiences and bring fresh perspectives to your content. When you team up with others, you not only diversify your video offerings but also learn from their experiences and strategies. Who knows? You might discover a new challenge idea or storytelling technique that could take your channel to the next level. Embrace the spirit of collaboration, and watch your community and creativity flourish.

Finally, keep a close eye on your analytics. These numbers are your compass in the ever-changing seas of YouTube. They reveal what works, what doesn't, and where your audience is most engaged. Use this data to refine your content strategy continuously. If a particular format or topic resonates well, lean into it; if not, don't be afraid to switch it up. Staying adaptable and responsive to your analytics will not only help you grow but will also ensure that you remain relevant and connected to your audience. So, gear up, stay playful, and let the waves of change carry you toward your goal of becoming the next Mr. Beast!

Staying True to Your Vision

Staying true to your vision is like having a trusty compass in the wild, guiding you through the chaos of YouTube stardom. When you step into the world of content creation, especially if you aspire to be the next Mr. Beast, it's easy to get sidetracked by trends, viral fads, and the pressure to conform. But remember, the magic happens when you embrace your unique perspective. Your vision is your secret sauce; it's what sets you apart from the sea of creators desperately chasing clicks and views. So, keep that vision front and center as you embark on your YouTube journey.

Imagine diving headfirst into a new video idea that's trending everywhere. Sure, it might promise a surge in views, but if it doesn't align with your core vision, you might find yourself feeling like a fish out of water. Instead, channel your inner Mr. Beast and think about what excites you. Whether that's creating jaw-dropping challenges, philanthropic endeavors, or simply sharing your quirky personality, staying true to what you love will resonate with your audience. They'll appreciate your authenticity, and that connection is what fuels loyalty and community.

Now, let's talk about the power of community. When you stick to your vision, you attract like-minded viewers who share your passions and interests. Building an engaging YouTube community is much easier when you're being genuine. Your subscribers will feel like they're part of something special, and that's where the real magic happens. The more your audience connects with your vision, the more likely they are to spread the word about your channel. This organic growth will ultimately lead to those viral moments you're chasing.

Don't shy away from collaboration, either! Working with other YouTubers can amplify your reach, but choose partners who align with your vision. Collaborating with creators who share your values will not only make the process more enjoyable but also foster authentic connections with their audiences. When everyone involved is passionate about the same vision, the energy will be contagious, resulting in content that feels cohesive and exciting for both sets of viewers.

Finally, let's touch on the importance of resilience. There will be times when the algorithm doesn't favor you, or your videos don't hit the mark, and that's completely normal. Staying true to your vision means weathering these storms with confidence. Use analytics to inform your decisions, but don't let them dictate your creativity. Remember, Mr. Beast didn't achieve success by playing it safe. He took risks and stayed committed to his vision, and that's a lesson every aspiring YouTuber should embrace. Keep creating, keep pushing boundaries, and most importantly, keep being you!

www.ingramcontent.com/pod-product-compliance
Lightning Source LLC
Chambersburg PA
CBHW070948210326
41520CB00021B/7106